ABT

ACPL ITEM
DISCARDED
ALLEN COUNTY PUBLIC LIBRARY
3 1833 03716

D0768793

n/00

Put Beginning Readers on the Right Track with
ALL ABOARD READING™

The All Aboard Reading series is especially for beginning readers. Written by noted authors and illustrated in full color, these are books that children really and truly *want* to read—books to excite their imagination, tickle their funny bone, expand their interests, and support their feelings. With four different reading levels, All Aboard Reading lets you choose which books are most appropriate for your children and their growing abilities.

Picture Readers—for Ages 3 to 6
Picture Readers have super-simple texts, with many nouns appearing as rebus pictures. At the end of each book are 24 flash cards—on one side is the rebus picture; on the other side is the written-out word.

Level 1—for Preschool through First-Grade Children
Level 1 books have very few lines per page, very large type, easy words, lots of repetition, and pictures with visual "cues" to help children figure out the words on the page.

Level 2—for First-Grade to Third-Grade Children
Level 2 books are printed in slightly smaller type than Level 1 books. The stories are more complex, but there is still lots of repetition in the text, and many pictures. The sentences are quite simple and are broken up into short lines to make reading easier.

Level 3—for Second-Grade through Third-Grade Children
Level 3 books have considerably longer texts, harder words, and more complicated sentences.

All Aboard for happy reading!

To Emily,
my soccer superstar—S.A.K.

To all the hard-working
women of America—K.C.

Allen County Public Library
900 Webster Street
PO Box 2270
Fort Wayne, IN 46801-2270

Photo credits: front cover, Todd Warshaw / Allsport; back cover, Elsa / Allsport; p. 1, Al Bello / Allsport; p. 5, Ezra Shaw / Allsport; p. 18-19, Al Bello / Allsport; p. 29, AP / Wide World Photos; p. 33, Elsa / Allsport; p. 37, Jed Jacobsohn / Allsport; p. 42, Ezra Shaw / Allsport; p. 43, Tom Hauck / Allsport; p. 44, Elsa / Allsport; p. 45, David Cannon / Allsport; p. 46, Ezra Shaw / Allsport; p. 47, Ezra Shaw / Allsport; p. 48, Reuters / Rick Wilson / Archive Photos.

Text copyright © 2000 by S.A. Kramer. Illustrations copyright © 2000 by Ken Call. All rights reserved. Published by Grosset & Dunlap, a division of Penguin Putnam Books for Young Readers, New York. ALL ABOARD READING is a trademark of The Putnam & Grosset Group. GROSSET & DUNLAP is a trademark of Grosset & Dunlap, Inc. Published simultaneously in Canada. Printed in the U.S.A.

Library of Congress Cataloging-in-Publication Data is available.

ISBN 0-448-42283-2 (GB)   A B C D E F G H I J
ISBN 0-448-42182-8 (pbk.)   A B C D E F G H I J

ALL
ABOARD
READING™

Level 3
Grades 2-3

U.S. Soccer Superstars

The Women Are Winners!

By S.A. Kramer
Illustrated by Ken Call
With photographs

Grosset & Dunlap • New York

The Big Game

It's Saturday, July 10, 1999, in Pasadena, California. The famous Rose Bowl stadium is jammed. A sellout crowd of 90,185 excited fans is ready to watch one of the most thrilling sports events of the year.

It's the Women's World Cup final. The United States women's soccer team is taking on China, its main rival. The American team is the most popular in women's sports history.

All across the U.S., people are talking about the match. Some of them don't understand soccer. Others don't even like the sport. It doesn't matter. This team has made everyone instant fans. That's why forty million TV sets are tuned to the game—the largest American audience ever to watch soccer.

It's easy to see why. The U.S. women are fearless and strong. With their talent and grit, they're among the best athletes in the world.

Fans adore them. Thousands turn out just to watch them practice. Girls follow them to their hotel, even into the bathroom. Children scream and squeal if they catch a mere glimpse of them.

No wonder the largest crowd ever to see a women's sports event has come out today. Families fill the seats. Kids have little American flags stuck in their hair. They've even painted their faces red, white, and blue to honor the team.

The famous have turned out too. The President is in the crowd. So are movie and TV stars. Two thousand reporters have showed up to cover the game.

How did one team make women's sports a prime-time event? Who are these athletes who have turned soccer into front-page news?

The Beginning

It wasn't always packed stadiums and screaming fans for Team USA. Just eight years ago, many people didn't realize women even played soccer. Crowds were small at most matches. Reporters ignored the sport. Games were never on radio or TV.

Even when the U.S. won the first Women's World Cup back in 1991, hardly anyone noticed. Few people paid attention when they lost the next Cup to

China in 1995. It seemed as if only the players cared about women and soccer.

The final game of the 1996 Olympics was a knock-down, drag-out fight, again against China. Star forward Mia Hamm was thrown to the ground eight times. She was so bruised and tired by the final minute, she had to be carried off the field in a stretcher. But the U.S. won, 2–1, when Tiffeny Milbrett scored the winning goal.

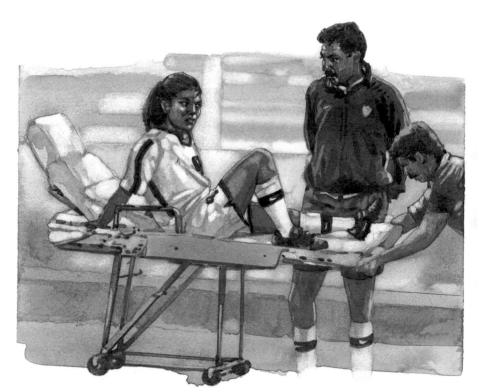

The crowd wouldn't stop cheering. The players were so happy, they rolled around in the grass. They accepted their gold medals holding hands while singing the national anthem.

It was their big moment—but no fan saw it on TV. Stations didn't show the game. They thought no one cared.

They were wrong. The club had won the country over. Plus, the sport of soccer had caught fire. Millions of girls were joining soccer clubs and leagues. And it was Team USA that they looked up to.

These twenty women weren't just great players—they were good people. They always signed autographs and applauded their fans. They weren't in the sport for money—they barely made enough to live on. The Nice Girls, as one magazine called them, played for the love of the game and the thrill of victory.

On this team, no one bragged or complained, or felt more important than her teammates. Unselfish athletes all, they shouted words of support to each other during a game. Together, they were showing America what true teamwork is.

So it was big news when the women's World Cup team was announced in January 1999. Everyone wanted to know, could the U.S. win another Cup? They'd

3 1833 03716 6326

have to beat the best to do it. China especially would be tough—they wanted revenge after the Olympics.

Each of the chosen women felt the pressure to succeed. They knew the whole world was watching. Would they come through?

Getting Ready

Orlando, Florida. Training camp opened on January 4, 1999. For the next six months, Team USA would live and work together. For the athletes, it was a big sacrifice. It meant they would see their loved ones just once a month.

The women knew practice was a key to victory. But teamwork was just as important. That's why they did special exercises to help them play as one.

In one exercise, the players lined up in a row and placed balloons between their bodies. Even when they moved, they had to keep the balloons afloat. There was only one way to do that—move together at exactly the same time.

To build up team trust, they tried something dangerous. Atop a high cliff, half the women put on blindfolds. Then the other half slowly helped them down.

They all reached the bottom safely. From then on their confidence in each other was that much stronger.

Each player was also given a videotape of her best moves. Called an "imaging" tape, it was set to her favorite music. The women watched these tapes over and over, and felt their faith in themselves rise.

At camp, soccer was the center of their lives. They spent most of the day together, practicing. Yet they never seemed to tire of each other's company.

The women played golf together. They went to movies and stuffed themselves on candy and frozen yogurt. Their favorite game was Scrabble. They even did jigsaw puzzles.

Over the months they grew closer and closer. Co-captain Julie Foudy kept them laughing with her jokes. Mia entertained them by mimicking Austin Powers. If they felt discouraged, co-captain Carla Overbeck got their spirits up. Midfielder Kristine Lilly realized they'd become a "second family."

Soon the coaches had to pick the starting eleven. The decision was tough, but their choices came as no surprise. Three forwards were named, instead of the more usual two. With Mia, Cindy

Parlow, and Tiffeny available, no coach could sit any of them down.

Quick-footed Mia was the first true superstar of women's soccer. No one, male or female, has scored more goals in international matches. Cindy was the team's youngest and tallest member. She had also won two national college player of the year awards. Speedy Tiffeny might have been little—she was the shortest on the club—but she was also its most reliable scorer.

The midfielders—Michelle Akers, Kristine, and Julie—were also very talented. In fact, Michelle's coach called her "the best woman who's ever played the game, period." The team's oldest and most important member, she could control the ball for the whole match. Tireless Kristine was judged by many to be the best all-round player in the world. She had appeared in more international matches than anyone else. Then there was quick-witted Julie, who could toe-poke the ball away from anyone.

The defenders, all four of them, were just as good. Muscular Brandi Chastain was the strongest athlete on the team. A student of the game, she could play almost every position. Fast-flying Kate

Sobrero made the toughest slide tackles look easy. Joy Fawcett was the club's best defender, with her great right foot and sneaky moves. Team leader Carla fired everyone up with her energy and her inspiring words.

The goalkeeper was Briana Scurry. With her nerves of steel, she made the eight-foot-high, twenty-four-foot-wide goal seem like a Ping-Pong net. "Being ice cold," she said, "is the way I do it."

US WOMEN \
MAY 2 2:00

The bench was full of stars, too. Shannon MacMillan, Tisha Venturini, Christie Pearce, Tracy Ducar, Lorrie Fair, Danielle Fotoupolos, Tiffany Roberts, Saskia Webber, and Sara Whalen were the all-important substitutes.

Now camp was over. The team had trained hard. Every athlete was ready to play. It was time for the Women's World Cup.

Going for the Cup

At first, June 19, 1999 could have been any other day. The team rose early in the morning and ate breakfast at 8 a.m. Then some of the women watched their imaging tapes. Others just showered, or packed a bag for the game.

But everyone knew this was no ordinary Saturday. At 3 p.m., the team would be in the Meadowlands, New Jersey, facing Denmark in the World Cup's opening match.

The women realized their fans had looked forward to this game for months. Still, when they walked onto the field, they were stunned to see a sellout crowd of 78,972. There were thousands dressed in team jerseys, waving flags and banners. The huge show of support brought lumps to their throats. It also made them nervous.

That's probably why they didn't play their best at the start. After just a few minutes, Mia realized she had to get the team going. Quickly, she went on the attack.

The crowd was behind her. Fans knew that Mia didn't always play well under pressure, even if she was soccer's top star. Once, a quiet Mia admitted, "I lack confidence."

Not today. With her brown ponytail bobbing behind her and her face fierce as a tiger's, Mia swept down the field, gliding around opponents. One teammate said, "It's like she's skating on ice with the ball." When Mia put it into the goal for the game's first score, the whole stadium went wild.

That's when the team relaxed. Julie and Kristine scored—and Briana shut

Denmark down for a 3–0 win. As the fans chanted "USA! USA!," the women took a victory lap. They jogged around the stadium applauding and thanking the crowd.

After the game, the team had a party with their families. Moms and dads, sisters and brothers, husbands and boyfriends—they'd all been watching from the stands. Kristine's grandmother was there, too. She slipped the star midfielder a dollar. She always gives her one for every goal she scores.

The U.S. was riding high. But Game Two started out badly. Before another sellout crowd, Nigeria scored in just sixty-two seconds. The Nigerians were playing rough, tough soccer. In sixteen minutes, they knocked Mia down from behind three times.

Mia was furious. So she did what she does best. Sprinting downfield, she took over the game. When she kicked a bullet from twenty yards out, it was goal and tie! She didn't stop there. Always a great passer, she got corner kicks and free kicks to teammates. She gave them confidence— and the ball. In just four minutes, the U.S. scored three goals.

Now the game was theirs. When it ended, it was a 7–1 win. Tiffeny called it "the most exciting game we've ever played."

The team barely had time to rest before they took on North Korea three days later. More than fifty thousand fans were in the seats in Foxboro, Massachusetts. They watched the bench score all the goals to take the game. The 3–0 U.S. victory was Briana's fifty-first shutout in ninety-three

matches. The coach said the goalkeeper was "like a rock of granite."

But despite Briana's dives and blocks in the next game, Team USA found themselves in big trouble. They were playing Germany in the quarterfinals in Washington, D.C. Just five minutes into the game, Brandi made a terrible pass. The team couldn't believe it—the ball

landed in the U.S. net. Brandi had accidentally scored for Germany!

The women were in shock. But they didn't stay down long. Neither did Brandi. Her husband says she "loves pressure situations." After a calm Tiffeny scored, Brandi sprang into action. Goal! Then Joy added another when she shot a header into the net. By the time the game was over, the U.S. had won, 3–2.

Fans around the country celebrated. But they also worried. The team seemed to be suffering from nerves. The defense had turned leaky, though once it had been as solid as a brick wall. If the women didn't get tough, they'd lose to Brazil in the semifinal.

Michelle wasn't about to let that happen. During the game with Brazil, she was bruised and kicked in the head. Her dad in the stands was afraid to watch in case she got hurt. But no injury could stop Michelle. She was a human tornado. She protected the ball with her headers, tackles, and passes, even scoring on a penalty kick.

The fans couldn't believe their eyes. They knew Michelle suffers from a disease called chronic fatigue syndrome. That means she often has terrible headaches and feels sick to her stomach. Sometimes she gets so tired and dizzy, she can't practice or play.

Yet when it counts, gutsy Michelle somehow gets herself out on the field. Mia says, "She's our hero." In the semifinal Michelle sparked the team to a 2–0 victory.

Briana had a great game, too—"the best...ever played," she commented. With her six saves, she punched one shot over the crossbar and stopped a breakaway that looked like a sure score.

So it was on to the final. It was the U.S. vs. China and the match wouldn't be easy. Just this year, the Chinese had beaten the U.S. twice. Crunch time was here. Would Team USA come out on top?

Champs!

The whistle blows. The clock starts ticking. The jam-packed Rose Bowl rocks with cheers. Down on the field it's boiling, but the athletes don't feel the heat. Kate says, "It's time to play and win this thing."

The action starts. The defense is holding tight. Plus there's Michelle. She's everywhere on the field. Diving for balls with her head, she makes all-important clears. At her best today, she even stops shots with her face. One reporter says that Michelle "owned the air."

The one thing she can't do is score. Neither can anyone else. The teams are so evenly matched, the game ends 0–0. But as overtime begins, Michelle can't go on. Not only is she hot and tired, she's also hurt her head. In the locker room, she lies down and breathes in oxygen through a mask.

It looks as if the U.S. will lose, and lose fast, without her. That's because the Chinese suddenly attack, letting loose a shot Briana can't reach. But as the ball zooms in, somehow Kristine leaps to block it. Arms out, eyes shut tight, she stops the kick with a header. Save!

Now the U.S. settles down. The Chinese don't score. But even after two overtimes, neither does Team USA. The game comes down to penalty kicks.

The clubs select five kickers each. They'll take turns trying to score. With the teams off the field, just one woman stands in the way—the goalkeeper.

The kickers get ready. They drink lots of water and have their legs massaged. On the sidelines, the U.S. is worried. Michelle's their best kicker, and she's out of the game.

But they have Briana. She feels it's up to her to get the win. She high-fives Kristine and tells the team, "I won't let you down."

At last it's time to play. The Chinese kick first. Briana can't stop the ball. Goal.

Now comes Carla, kicking first for the U.S. As she approaches the penalty stripe twelve yards out, all hearts beat faster. She moves to her right, kicks—and scores! 1–1.

The Chinese get another goal, then Joy answers off a stutter step. With the score

2–2, the next Chinese kicker comes to the stripe.

This time Briana has a hunch. She thinks the kicker will go left. Diving in that direction, she stretches her whole body off the ground. She's guessed right! With her fingertips, she bats the ball away. She says later, "I knew that I had to make one save."

But the game's not over. The U.S. must score. Kristine blasts a shot into the goal. Team USA has the lead!

Not for long. China evens the score on the very next kick. Now it's Mia's turn. To get the lead back, she has to put the ball in.

But she's exhausted. Even worse, she hates to take penalty kicks. A few minutes ago, she asked the coach if Shannon could shoot instead. Yet when Mia comes to the stripe, she pulls herself together. She rockets the ball into the right corner. Goal!

China doesn't give up. They even the score. Now there's one chance left to win, or a new penalty round begins. Brandi, the last kicker, must get a goal.

The fans are screaming. They can't believe it's come down to this. At midfield, the U.S. women stand together arm in arm. They look as if they're praying.

All week long, Brandi's been practicing for this moment. Now she's concentrating so hard, she doesn't even hear the crowd cheering. She and her coach have discussed a plan. Brandi knows the goalkeeper expects her to kick with her strong right foot. Instead she'll use the weaker left, and fool her.

The whistle blows. "I just stepped up and hit it," she says. The ball sails into the upper right-hand corner. Goal!

The crowd goes crazy. Brandi falls to her knees. Ripping off her shirt, she twirls it over her head triumphantly. She says later, "I thought, this is the greatest moment of my life on a soccer field! I just lost my head."

Her teammates surround her. There are smiles, hugs, and tears all around. Michelle stumbles out of the locker room to join the celebration. As Cindy proudly raises the World Cup high, confetti sprays down from the stands. It seems as if everyone in the stadium is sharing in the joy.

One person's missing, though. Briana's disappeared. Overcome by emotion, she's gone off to a corner of the field to cry. But she's weeping from happiness. Her team is number one!

Celebrating

The U.S. women's team has made
history. Just as important, they've won
the hearts of millions of Americans. They
have become national heroes.

No wonder the President visits them in
the locker room after the game. He
thanks the players "for the gift you have
given the United States." The women are
so happy, they pour champagne over his
head!

That night, they throw a party at a
fancy hotel. They and their loved ones

dance until morning. Kristine, named the game's Most Spectacular Player, ends up with an extra prize—a dollar from her grandmother for the penalty kick she scored.

It seems all of America wants to celebrate with the team. So they go to Disneyland for a parade, and then on to rallies in Los Angeles and New York. They can hardly believe it when they see themselves on the covers of magazines. They get even more excited when they appear on national TV. Then the White House calls. They're so popular, the President wants to see them again!

But this is a team that doesn't let fame go to their heads. Playing great soccer is what matters to them. That's why they'll always remember 1999. As Kristine says, their victory "will go down in our hearts forever."

Brandi Chastain

5'7", 130 lbs.

Birthday: July 21, 1968

Nickname: Hollywood, because she's so dramatic

As a little girl, Brandi loved tap dancing, ballet, and Little League—but soccer topped them all. She spent hours in front of her house just practicing her footwork. As an adult, she's been every bit as dedicated, even postponing her honeymoon to play in the Olympics. She constantly studies videotapes of games to learn new moves. Now she can play nearly every position. She's also a fitness fanatic, with "bigger biceps and shoulders," she says, "than my dad."

Julie Foudy

5'6", 130 lbs.

Birthday: January 23, 1971

Nickname: Jules, or Loudy, because she's a chatterbox

"If I was quiet," Julie says, "people would think something was wrong." It's true that she talks a lot, but she has something to say. She is the conscience of the team. It was Julie who made sure Team USA's soccer balls weren't made by companies using children as workers.

Smart and confident, Julie's been accepted to medical school. But she'll try to be a sportscaster instead of a doctor, since that's her childhood dream.

Briana Scurry

5'8", 150 lbs.

Birthday: September 7, 1971

Nickname: The Rock, because her nerve never fails

Football was Briana's favorite sport as a girl. But after she joined a soccer club at the age of nine, she couldn't stay away from the game. As a teenager, she even became a referee. Knowing the rules inside out helped make her a great goalkeeper. So did learning to stay cool on the field. But Briana has a hidden wild side. Before the '96 Olympics, she vowed that if the team won, she'd jog naked down the street. So at 2:07 in the morning she took a run in nothing but her gold medal!

Kristine Lilly

5'4", 125 lbs.

Birthday: July 22, 1971

Nickname: Lil

Maybe it was all those games with her brother and five male cousins, but by six, Kristine had learned soccer. By sixteen, she was on the national team.

Now she's one of the fittest athletes in the sport. As one of her teammates says, "She can run all day." But for Kristine soccer isn't just about the body. She believes it's a game for the mind, too. That's why one of her favorite things to do is just sit and think about the sport.

Michelle Akers

5'10", 150 lbs.

Birthday: February 1, 1966

Nickname: Mufasa, for her leadership and her mane

She may often be ill, but Michelle is as tough as they come. She gets so carried away by her will to win that she gets more penalties than any of her teammates. Not even having had twelve knee operations can keep her off the field. No wonder she's the heart and soul of the team.

It's not surprising she's so spunky—she takes after her mom, a firefighter.

Tiffeny Milbrett

5'2", 130 lbs.

Birthday: October 23, 1972

Nickname: Millie

Tiffeny's always been a great athlete. By eight, she was playing stand-out soccer. In high school, she was a track and basketball star. Now most coaches expect her to become a soccer superstar. But Tiffeny just may surprise them—she wants to play in the WNBA. She may be short, but she's a deadly passer, and has great bursts of speed. "People tell me," she proudly comments, "my first three steps look like an explosion." If anyone can make her dream come true, it's Tiffeny. As one teammate says, she's a "fireball."

Mia Hamm

5'5", 125 lbs.

Birthday: March 17, 1972

Mia's mom wanted her to be a ballerina. But one of her brothers taught her to play soccer when she was only five. As she got older, he encouraged modest Mia to become a star. It worked—at fifteen, she was the youngest woman ever to make the national team. Now she's such a great player that one coach says, "When she gets the ball, you hold your breath." In her magical career, only one thing's gone wrong. Her brother died at the age of twenty-eight, and Mia misses him terribly. She wears his initials on her soccer shoes, to honor his memory.